Keeping Pet
CHICKENS

Keeping Pet
CHICKENS

*Bring your garden to life and enjoy
the bounty of fresh eggs from your own
small flock of happy hens*

JOHANNES PAUL AND WILLIAM WINDHAM

Interpet Publishing

Published by Interpet Publishing,
Vincent Lane, Dorking,
Surrey RH4 3YX,
England

© 2005 Interpet Publishing Ltd.
This reprint 2007
ISBN 978-1-84286-103-5

Credits

Editor: Philip de Ste. Croix
Designer: Phil Clucas MSIAD
Studio photography: Neil Sutherland
Diagram artwork: Martin Reed
Production management: Consortium, Poslingford, Suffolk
Print production: SNP Leefung, China
Printed and bound in the Far East

The Authors

Johannes Paul was born in Sussex in 1978 and grew up on a small farm with many animals including pigs, goats, horses and chickens. After studying Mechanical Engineering at Brunel University, he gained a Masters in Product Design from the Royal College of Art in London. Together with three friends he founded Omlet in order to encourage more people to keep chickens. Omlet produces the eglu – a modern chicken house suitable for a small garden that makes keeping chickens easy and fun.

William Windham was born in Norwich in 1978 and lived in the deepest Norfolk countryside for the next 20 years. He studied Engineering at Cambridge University and Industrial Design at the Royal College of Art. Since graduating he has concentrated on the Omlet company supplying people with chicken houses and a little of the good life. Chickens are central to his day's work – just walking into the studio in the morning involves tripping over at least ten chickens!

The recommendations in this book are given without any guarantees on the part of the author and publisher. If in doubt, seek the advice of a vet or pet-care specialist.

Contents

INTRODUCTION

An unusual and rewarding pet

Friendly, interesting and inexpensive to keep, chickens can be kept in most gardens with only simple equipment needed to house them. It is not necessary to have a cockerel; indeed, unless you have very understanding neighbours, it is not advised. Your chickens will lay eggs just as happily without one. As chickens are social animals, they should be kept in pairs or more and they respond well to human contact. With undemanding care and attention these intriguing pets will provide you with delicious fresh eggs and a lot of entertainment.

Chickens have been around a long time.

The first chickens lived around 5000 BC in the jungles of South Asia and were called Red Jungle Fowl. Roosting high up in the trees, they had large talons and strong beaks and were very much like a bird of prey. There is evidence that there were also early types of

chickens in other parts of the world. In South America, the Arauca Indians bred a chicken that laid blue eggs, called the Araucana. Its purity was fiercely guarded by the Arauca and it is still bred today.

As trade between different countries and continents increased, chickens spread across the world, merchants often bringing home unusual and pretty chickens from far away countries as presents for their wives and families.

Left: You don't need a vast estate to keep chickens. Virtually every garden can accommodate a pair.

Domestication and breeding

The Ancient Egyptians developed the technique for hatching chickens artificially, and this was the beginning of the mass domestication of chickens for food and eggs. The Ancient Greeks valued the strength and beauty of the cockerel and it became a symbol for bravery. Used for sport in cockfighting, cockerels were also sacrificed to the gods. Most households kept chickens for their eggs. When Queen Victoria was given some chickens, their popularity in Britain took off. Cockfighting was outlawed, and the Victorians set up clubs and held shows where people could display their chickens in competitions, a tradition which continues to this day.

HANDY HINTS

Below: Domesticated chickens have lived their lives alongside humankind for thousands of year.

ROYAL CHICKENS
Queen Victoria was given Cochin chickens, a large heavy breed from China which have feathery legs that make them look as if they are wearing trousers. When people first saw them they were fascinated by these enormous birds, the likes of which they had never seen before.

CHICKENS ARE EVERYWHERE!
The Warner Bros. cartoon character Foghorn Leghorn and the animated film Chicken Run in which some ill-fated chickens plot their escape from the Tweedy poultry farm are just a couple of recent examples of the universal popularity of chickens. Our language itself is infused with chicken references – think about having a hen party, being hen-pecked, feeling broody, having something to crow about and ruling the roost. And don't count your chickens…!

DIFFERENT AGES, DIFFERENT NAMES
You can call a chicken a chicken regardless of its age or sex, but there are special names as well. Before she lays her first egg a female chicken is called a pullet; after that she becomes a hen. A young male chicken is called a cockerel; when fully grown he is known as a cock.

BASIC ANATOMY

The head

A chicken has an incredible-looking head compared to many birds. The fleshy comb on the top of the head comes in many different shapes from big and floppy 'single' combs to small and spiky 'rose' combs. The comb and the smaller fleshy protuberances under the beak called the wattles generally become slightly larger and redder as the chicken comes into lay. With its keen close-range eyesight a chicken can use its beak to pick up grains of corn with amazing accuracy. But the chicken doesn't chew them; it has no teeth – hence the saying 'as rare as hen's teeth'. If you look closely at the beak, you will also notice two nostrils near the back edge.

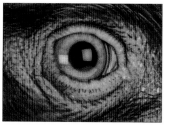

Left: Chickens have an extremely well-developed sense of sight; their vision is more acute than a human's.

The feathers that cover the body of a fully grown bird account for around five per cent of its live weight.

A special vocabulary is used to describe the various parts of a chicken. Try to memorize the terms shown on this annotated photograph.

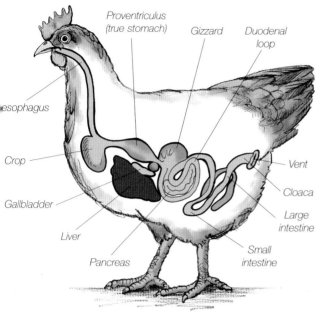

Proventriculus
(true stomach)   Gizzard   Duodenal
loop

Oesophagus

Crop

Gallbladder

Liver

Pancreas

Vent

Cloaca

Large
intestine

Small
intestine

Digestion

Food is sent on its way down the oesophagus by a pointy tongue. The first stop is the crop, a pouch that holds and softens food. If you pick up your chicken at the end of the day, you will be able to feel a roughly golf-ball-sized lump on the front of its chest. This is the crop full of the day's food. Next the soft food passes through the proventriculus where digestive acid and enzymes are added and on to the gizzard, a muscular organ where food is ground up. Any insoluble grit the chicken has picked up helps the food to be ground up in the gizzard. The rest of the process takes place in the intestines where all the nutrients and water are absorbed before waste matter leaves the chicken through the vent (right).

HANDY HINTS

BASIC ANATOMY

The limbs

Chickens aren't very good at flying. Smaller breeds can achieve some impressive flapping jumps, but the heavier breeds never come close to taking off. The wings are made up of several sets of feathers, the large ones at the front of the wing being the primary flight feathers. They may not be good in the air but most chickens can run faster than you would expect! A few breeds have feathers on their legs but most chickens' legs and feet are just covered in scales that provide good protection against all the digging around that they do. At the end of their legs are toes with nails that they keep short by scratching in the dirt.

Shank

Toenail

Scales

Above: The scales on the shanks are made of specialized skin cells. In hot weather increased blood flow through the legs helps birds to keep cool.

Secondary flight feathers (18)

Right: Feathers help to insulate a bird and to aid it in flight. While chickens are not very able fliers, they can usually travel a short distance by flapping their wings, so you must make sure that any outside runs are secure to keep them safely inside.

Primary flight feathers (10)

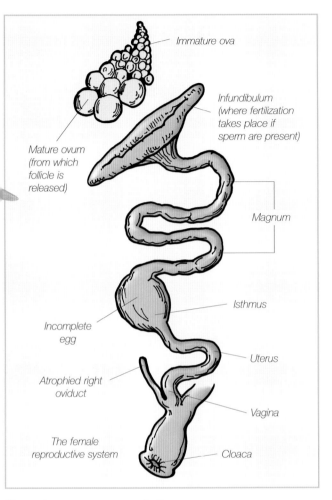

- Immature ova
- Infundibulum (where fertilization takes place if sperm are present)
- Mature ovum (from which follicle is released)
- Magnum
- Isthmus
- Incomplete egg
- Atrophied right oviduct
- Uterus
- Vagina
- The female reproductive system
- Cloaca

How is an egg made?

A chicken's body contains lots of tiny undeveloped follicles (yolks) which slowly grow one by one to the size we recognize as an egg yolk. When a follicle is ready, a yolk is released from the ovary and travels down a section of the oviduct (the magnum) where it is attached to and coated in egg white. Next, in the isthmus, thin membranes form around the white and the egg then moves down to the uterus where the shell forms. The last stages see colour and a protective layer called the cuticle being added. The egg is now ready to be laid! From start to finish the whole process takes around 25 hours.

PURE BREEDS

Various types of chicken

Chickens come in hundreds of types and colours. They are basically classified according to their breed. Individual breeds can contain several different varieties that are distinguished by different markings and colourings. Pure breeds are birds of a single breed that is recognized by the official national organizations that govern the standards and regulations that apply to poultry. Standard breeds are the familiar medium to large chickens, while bantams (see pages 22-25) are smaller, lighter birds. In addition to purebred stock, there are also hybrids (see pages 18-21) which have been developed by crossing two breeds to create a new strain. This is normally done for commercial reasons to create birds which will lay more eggs or produce more meat than pure breeds. Hybrids may not look as gorgeous as some of the highly decorative pure breeds, but they are reliable and productive birds that are eminently suitable for the home chicken keeper.

Barnevelder

The Barnevelder was named after the Dutch town of Barneveld, which lies about 50km southwest of the capital Amsterdam. This was the centre of egg production in Holland in the early 20th century. A particularly well-balanced chicken, the Barnevelder has large bright orange eyes and really yellow legs and beak. Her solid, broad body is covered in feathers in alternating loops of russet brown and greeny black. If not kept fit by having plenty of space for exercise, she can become lazy, but otherwise she will lead an active life and will lay approximately 200 caramel brown eggs per year.

Above: Laced Barnevelders have a beautifully subtle plumage that combines dark green-black feathers with a deep red-brown hue.

Left: The single comb is typically rather small; earlobes are red.

Wheaten Maran

Beautiful honey-coloured feathers, grace and poise characterize the Wheaten Maran (below). She becomes very tame if handled frequently and will always come running across the garden if she suspects you are bringing her some titbits from the kitchen! The Wheaten is one type of the French Maran breed, others are the dark Cuckoo and the Copper Black. In common with the other Marans, she is a consistent layer of large chestnut-coloured eggs and you can expect around 200 per year. Her big soft feathers are perfect for sitting on the nest and, indeed, she makes a good mother.

HANDY HINTS

WONDERFUL VARIETY

If you are new to chicken keeping and assume that all chickens look more or less the same, think again. Chickens come in a dazzling array of colours, varieties and styles of plumage.

PURE BREEDS

Rhode Island Red

The Rhode Island Red is the famous brown egg-laying hen seen on farmyards all over the world. It originated in Little Compton in the American state of Rhode Island at the beginning of the 19th century. It is a strong and vigorous breed that is capable of laying 260 eggs per year. This is more than any other pure-breed hen. As a result the Rhode Island Red was used as the basis for creating many of the hybrid or crossbreed hens popular today in commercial egg-producing farms. They do make good pets as well, but are happiest with plenty of space to range. In 1954 this chicken was adopted as the official state bird of Rhode Island, USA.

Right: The Rhode Island Red's striking glossy plumage is a rich chestnut-red in colour.

Left: These are easy-going and hardy birds that are well suited to a backyard or garden.

Light Sussex

The Light Sussex often takes the top honours at shows and with her pretty black lacing and polar white body leading to a final flourish of black tail feathers, it's easy to see why. Of the pure-breed hens only the Rhode Island Red can rival the Sussex for the number of eggs she lays, up to 260 per year. The eggs are cream to light brown-coloured. The docile Sussex hen (there are other colours such as silver) is quite happy being kept in a town garden. There is also a bantam version which is just as attractive but lays smaller eggs.

Note the prominent comb and wattles and light-coloured legs

Right: The combination of white body plumage and black neck and tail feathers means that Light Sussex hens look very striking. However, they do tend to get rather dirty when kept outside in wet conditions.

HANDY HINTS

PURE BREEDS

Buff Orpington

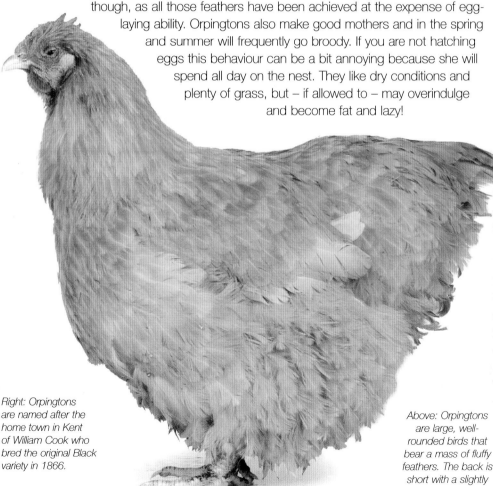

Many people are drawn to the Buff Orpington because of her spectacular mass of fluffy feathers. They make good pets as they are docile and are not good at flying because they have small wings. Don't expect many eggs though, as all those feathers have been achieved at the expense of egg-laying ability. Orpingtons also make good mothers and in the spring and summer will frequently go broody. If you are not hatching eggs this behaviour can be a bit annoying because she will spend all day on the nest. They like dry conditions and plenty of grass, but – if allowed to – may overindulge and become fat and lazy!

Right: Orpingtons are named after the home town in Kent of William Cook who bred the original Black variety in 1866.

Above: Orpingtons are large, well-rounded birds that bear a mass of fluffy feathers. The back is short with a slightly concave shape.

Below: Welsummers are a hardy and attractive breed that generally thrive under free-range conditions. Typically they display a black-red pattern while the breast is a rich chestnut red. There is also a bantam form.

FINE FEATHERS

The copious feathering that is characteristic of the Orpington breed was achieved by selective breeding in the Victorian era. As well as buff, they come in black, blue and white varieties.

EYE-CATCHING EGGS

Welsummers are particularly prized for their dark-brown eggs which are sometimes described as flowerpot-coloured. The eggs can have a variety of speckling and sometimes even look textured.

Welsummer

Some chickens are bred for their feathers, some for their size and some for the colour of their eggs. The Welsummer was created by cross-breeding many different chickens including: the Partridge Cochin, Barnevelder, Rhode Island Red and Partridge Leghorn. This resulted in a highly prized terracotta-coloured egg, and the Welsummer also has very attractively coloured feathers. A popular chicken which is happy being kept in a back garden, the Welsummer, which originated in the village of Welsum in Holland, will lay around 200 eggs per year.

Right: The hackle feathers of the female Welsummer have a glorious iridescent sheen and reveal a striping pattern that is missing from the males. The combs are smallish and firm-set, earlobes are red and the shanks are yellow. They are generally docile birds with a nice disposition.

HYBRID VARIETIES

More eggs

Although the pure breeds can look beautiful with amazing feathers and combs, they tend to sacrifice performance for looks. Cross-breeding two or more pure-breed hens can result in a chicken that not only looks good but also lays a super number of eggs. These birds are called hybrid or crossbreed chickens and can be found on free-range chicken farms all over the world.

Right: Hybrids have been developed commercially to maximize egg-laying or meat-producing ability. Hybrids are popular with first-time chicken keepers and make affectionate pets.

Over the years people have created crossbreeds which make excellent pets for the first-time chicken owner because of their friendly nature and ability to lay consistently well. Breeders will often give the crossbreeds their own particular names, so it is best to ask about the particular characteristics of the chicken that you are interested in.

Rhode Island Red-based hybrids

There are many hybrids to choose from with most
laying in the region of 300 eggs a year.
Lots of them are based on the
Rhode Island Red, a dark brown
pure-breed chicken that lays
around 250 eggs per year.
Crossing the Rhode Island
Red with other breeds –
such as the Light
Sussex, Marans and
Plymouth Rock –
has produced lots of differently
coloured hybrids that will lay you almost an egg every day.
The cross-breeding also results in differently coloured
eggs. Crossing with a Maran produces a slightly darker
egg than usual, a pale chestnut brown. Spending time
with these chickens is soon
rewarded as they become
amazingly tame and
comfortable with human
contact.

HANDY HINTS

PEACE OF MIND
*Buying hybrids from a breeder
is a good way of ensuring that
you have purchased hardy,
healthy birds. Vaccination is a
relatively expensive procedure
but the larger producers do it
as a matter of course.*

DO A GOOD DEED
*Some people have set up
schemes to rescue battery hens.
Although they may look worse
for wear, these poor chickens
still have a lot to give and by
buying them you can ensure
they live out the rest of their
days in relative luxury.*

White Star

Although most of the
hybrids are good
layers, there are other
appealing
characteristics to look
out for. The White
Star (right) is a
beautiful looking
chicken with the most
amazing big floppy red comb
due to its Leghorn ancestry. It lays
a good number of pure white eggs
but takes much longer to get used to
human contact. It can be quite skittish, although
it can be highly amusing seeing it make cartoon-
style sprints across the garden!

HYBRID VARIETIES

Black Rock

The Black Rock was produced in America and is one of the most successful crossbred chickens. Bred from specially selected strains of Rhode Island Red cockerels and Plymouth Rock females, the hens are friendly, not easily stressed by being handled and superb egg layers. In the right conditions, they will lay up to 320 eggs per year. They have thick plumages, don't mind getting a bit wet and enjoy human company – so much so that they quite often follow their owner through the back door and into the kitchen if given a chance to do so.

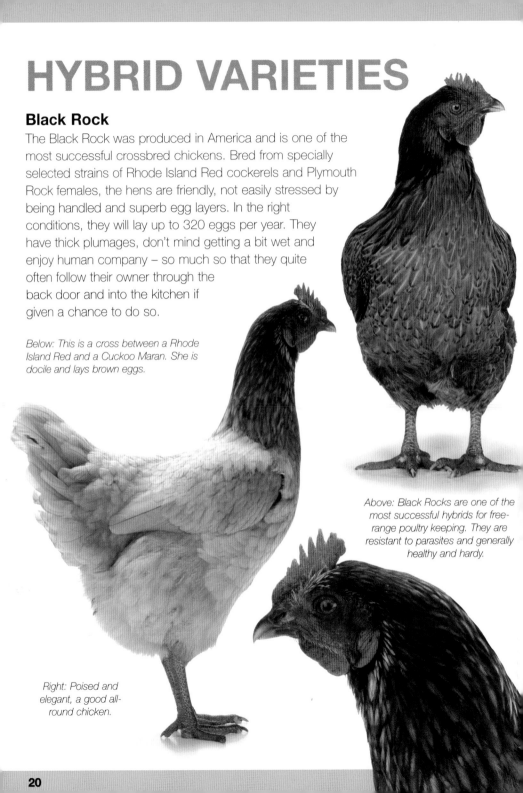

Below: This is a cross between a Rhode Island Red and a Cuckoo Maran. She is docile and lays brown eggs.

Above: Black Rocks are one of the most successful hybrids for free-range poultry keeping. They are resistant to parasites and generally healthy and hardy.

Right: Poised and elegant, a good all-round chicken.

Speckledy hen

Speckledy hens are very attractive hybrid chickens (Rhode Island Red crossed with Maran) that make excellent garden pets. They have white legs and barred dark grey and white feathers with a good sized comb and wattles. A Speckledy chicken will lay around 250 eggs per year and because they are bred from the French Maran hen lay a very dark brown egg. They look very similar to a purebred Maran and share quite a lot of its characteristics, such as being active, graceful and placid. They are quite heavy chickens and will eat quite a lot compared to other breeds.

HANDY HINTS

LESS EXPENSIVE
Hybrids tend to be cheaper than pure breeds. Expect a hybrid to cost around £5 to £10 while a pure breed will cost anything upwards of £20

DON'T BE FOOLED
Breeders will often try to sell a trio, this means a cockerel and two hens. If a pair of chickens is advertised, this will be a male and a female. Don't forget though that if your chickens hatch a clutch of chicks, around 60 per cent will be cockerels and you ought not to keep more than one cockerel with your hens because otherwise males will fight.

SEX-LINKED CHICKS
When browsing thorough classified advertisements offering chicks for sale, you may see the term 'sex-link'. This refers to the practice of breeding hybrids that can be immediately sexed at hatching, usually by the colour of the male and female chicks' down, or sometimes by their feather development.

Right: The Speckledy, a Maran/Rhode Island Red cross, can produce around 250 dark brown eggs a year.

BANTAMS

The advantages of bantams

Bantams are a great choice if your garden space is restricted as their small size means that they can live in a smaller area than standard-sized chickens. A number of bantams have been bred as miniature versions of standard breeds, but 'true bantams' have no large equivalent – they are naturally small in size. It all depends on the breed but they are often no larger than a pigeon in size. Because of their light weight, they can be quite good fliers. A lot of the breeds make excellent mothers but, if you are not breeding from them, this broodiness can be a nuisance as they will not lay any eggs for weeks.

Above: Pekins are characterized by the extraordinary covering of feathers that grow on their hocks. This is a Buff Pekin.

Pekin bantam

Very popular as a pet because of its size, looks and character, Pekins have been bred in many different colours, including black, buff, dark grey, lavender, white, gold, partridge and cuckoo (stripy). Their feathers are long and soft and extend all the way down the legs giving them a comical appearance as though they are wearing trousers. They don't lay many eggs though, about 60 a year is normal. They are particularly suitable for very small gardens.

Below: The high tail and short legs are typical of the Japanese bantam, which is a very ancient breed.

HANDY HINTS

CHICKENS MAKE GOOD SAILORS
Pekin bantams were first brought to Europe from China after the Anglo-French armies destroyed the Summer Palace in Peking in 1860. Originally thought to be a miniature version of the Cochin also from China, Pekins are know thought to be a true bantam.

EXOTIC NAME
The word bantam comes from the village of Bantam in Java. After a trading boat from the East Indies arrived in England carrying lots of miniature chickens, the Victorians used the name to denote any small chicken.

Japanese bantam
Chickens originated in the Far East, and so the Japanese have a long history of breeding chickens with particular characteristics. The most striking feature of the Japanese bantam is its tail which is large and upright. Pronounced in the female, it is really spectacular in the male. They have very short legs and so prefer dry, short grass but otherwise are easy to look after. This is a true bantam with no standard version.

BANTAMS

Polish bantam (chamois- and silver-laced varieties)

Rather confusingly the Polish is thought to have originated in Italy where it is prized for its outrageous puffy hairdo, but the breed was perfected in Holland. There are eight recognized varieties of Polish and some have a beard of feathers under their beaks as well as the crest of feathers on their heads. They are very popular as they are good egg layers as well as being very easy to pick up and tame because they can't see you coming! They are harder to keep clean and you must be vigilant for lice and mites which can live in the crest.

Silver-laced (below); chamois (bottom).

Right: The crest of the Polish bantam should be as large and globe-shaped as possible; the comb is hidden under it.

Maran bantam

The Maran originates from France and the eggs are prized for their colour, a beautiful dark mahogany brown. The bantam version of the breed lays extremely well, even better than the standard size (see page 13) which is prone to overeating and laziness. Very pretty and hardy, they are bright, active chickens.

Above: The Maran is not a 'true' bantam, but a miniature version of a standard breed.

LADIES ONLY
Because most bantams do not lay very many eggs and are not large enough to eat, they have traditionally been kept as pets. In fact they used to be considered only suitable for women to look after!

SMALLER PORTIONS
Bantams lay small eggs, normally they are only half the size of a standard chicken's egg. So while they are greatly prized for their ornamental qualities, their contribution to the kitchen pantry is not their strongest point.

TRADITIONAL CHICKEN HOUSES

The design is important

Chickens' housing requirements are quite simple as they tend to spend most of their time outside. The house is used basically for laying eggs, sleeping or as a shelter in bad weather. It is quite possible to build your own house using materials available in most DIY shops or you can buy a ready-made one. Most houses you can buy are made of wood. They usually come with a run attached to the house. The basic requirements are a perch to sleep on, a nesting box and security from predators. When building or buying a house, you should also consider how many chickens you are going to keep, how easy it is to clean and how easy it is to move.

Both right:
Larger chicken houses
are available if you want to
keep more than just two or
three birds. These designs are
suitable for 6-10 birds (lower)
and up to 15 chickens (upper).

Above: Simple wooden chicken houses suitable for the garden should have a secure door which can be locked at night when the birds have gone in to roost. Predators pose a continual threat to chickens.

Security

The house should be secure against all types of vermin including foxes, badgers and rats. Be sure that there are no easy access holes through which these unwelcome visitors can get in. The door that the chickens use to go in and out should have a strong lock as a persistent animal like a fox will often work out how to open a simple catch. If there is another door for collecting eggs, make sure that too is secure.

TRADITIONAL
CHICKEN HOUSES

Perches

The perch should be a 25-35mm wide bar that the chickens can grip comfortably with their feet. The edges should be rounded and it should be positioned towards the back of the house. If there is more than one perch, they should all be at the same height, and not too high as the chickens can injure themselves jumping off. Some large heavy chickens may not use a perch but be more happy sleeping on the floor. As chickens do about half their droppings at night, position a removable tray underneath the perches – it makes keeping the house clean a lot easier.

House and nesting box area

Entrance protected by sliding door

Area of enclosed run

Above and left: There are a range of arks on the market that can accommodate different numbers of birds. They feature a traditional enclosed chicken house with a run attached to it. Birds get in and out of the run by means of a door in the front of the house.

Nesting boxes

Your house should have at least one nesting box per four chickens, as they will take it in turns to lay. The nesting box can either be inside or sometimes mounted outside the house. You can use straw, dust-free wood shavings or even shredded paper to line the nesting box. Never use hay as this can develop a mould that can cause your chickens health problems. If there is a door or flap in the side of the house near the nestbox, it will make collecting the eggs much more convenient.

Left: This larger house can hold up to 24 laying hens.
1 Roof to nesting box area.
2 Sliding door.
3 Side wall (removable for cleaning).
4 Removable tiered perches.
5 Bank of nesting boxes.
6 Partition between nesting boxes.

HOUSEPROUD
Remember to keep your wooden chicken house in good condition by treating it once a year with a safe wood preservative, not only to keep it looking good but to prevent it from becoming weakened by the weather and so liable to rot. Keep the birds well away while you do this and let the stain dry thoroughly.

Above: Cleaning out the droppings from your chicken house is an unpleasant, but very necessary, chore.

KEEPING IT CLEAN
When selecting a chicken house, if possible choose a design that allows you to take the inside of the house apart, and remove all the internal fittings, for regular cleaning. Mites like to live in the cracks at the end of roosting bars and if you can't remove them, they will be difficult to clean properly.

A 21ST-CENTURY CHICKEN HOUSE

The innovative eglu

This is a brand new type of chicken house designed specifically for the first-time owner. It provides everything that two chickens need for sleeping and laying eggs. Inside there are two main areas, the nesting box and the roosting area. When chickens sleep they like to grip on to a perch, rather like a branch of a tree. The floor is made of wooden bars allowing the chickens to choose where they sleep. They don't need any straw where they roost but you can put some in the nesting box. The chickens will take it in turns during the day to lay their eggs, but they like privacy so try not to peek!

Easy to clean

The smooth plastic surfaces of this chicken house are very easy to clean. A soft brush and a household disinfectant can be used to clean the inside – scrubbing the unit once a month will make sure that your chickens have a hygienic home. The roost bars are also removable leaving nasty parasites such as red-mite (which love nooks and crannies) nowhere to hide. All the droppings the chickens do inside fall through the roost bars onto the droppings tray. The tray then simply slides out allowing you to carry the droppings to the compost heap.

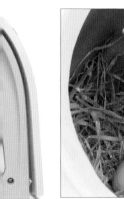

Behind closed doors

The eglu keeps the chickens warm in the winter and cool in the summer in the same way that double glazing works in your house. An air gap between two layers keeps the inside temperature constant. The front door can be opened and closed using the handle on the top. It locks too, so at night the house is a cosy, secure retreat for the chickens. In the morning when you open the door the chickens will come rushing out looking for breakfast. You might find yours too, freshly laid in the nesting box!

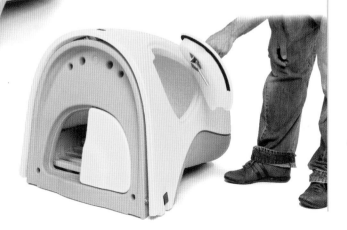

HANDY HINTS

MOVING HOUSE
When you go on holiday and need to take your chickens to a friend's house, it is simple to transport the chickens securely inside the unit. Try to keep travelling time to a minimum, especially when it is hot. Chickens don't mind being shut in for a few hours at a time, but try to keep stress to a minimum.

LET THE LIGHT IN
Once you have cleaned the inside, leave the lid off for a few hours to let some sunlight in. The UV rays will kill off many micro-organisms that prefer hiding away in dark moist places. It pays to do this about once a month.

NO MAINTENANCE
Unlike a wooden house, this design doesn't require any long-term maintenance. Wooden houses need to be treated or painted every year but plastic only needs regular washing and cleaning.

THE RUN

Small runs

Depending on whether you have a small urban garden or a large garden in the countryside, you will probably have a different way of keeping your chickens. Many chicken houses come with a run attached to them which some people keep their chickens in all the time. Others use it as a secure area to keep the chickens in when they are not around. If you are going to be keeping your birds in a run for most of the time, your chickens should preferably have over 1 square metre of space each.

Above: Chickens need time to scratch around in the outside world. A run affords them security as they do so.

Mesh skirt to deter tunelling predators

Above: The eglu is provided with a secure wire run that attaches to the front of the chicken house.

Large runs

An alternative to keeping a small run and letting your chickens out to roam anywhere they please is to section off an area of the garden around their house. If you decide to do this, make sure that it is properly secure. Remember that foxes can climb so don't forget a roof! The grass will soon wear thin if you keep the chickens in one place so putting bark chippings down is a great alternative. A small run can be moved to a new area of grass to keep it fresh and disease-free while bark chippings can be simply raked out and a new layer spread every month or so.

Protecting your run

There are several ways to stop animals from tunnelling into your chicken run. You can excavate and bury the netting some way into the ground so that any tunnelling attempt is thwarted. However, this has the drawback of preventing the run being moved around easily. Alternatively you can construct your run with netting on all sides including the bottom, although this makes the floor area more difficult to clean. Or you can make your run with a 'skirt' of meshing not less than

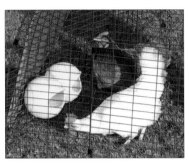

Above: Feeders and drinkers can easily be situated in a run so that the chickens have ready access to food and water whenever they need it.

20cm wide all round. This stops predators like foxes digging under the base of the run wall while still enabling you to move the run easily while keeping the birds protected.

Below: A house with a run attached to it can easily be moved around the garden – your grass will appreciate this!

HANDY HINTS

ADD INTEREST

You can do many things to make life more interesting for chickens that stay in a run most of the time. Hang up old broccoli stalks for them to peck at. Don't hang them so that they have to jump to reach them though as this could upset their egg laying. If you put a mirror up, your birds will spend a surprising amount of time looking at themselves.

Broccoli makes a welcome treat.

MESH SIZE AND MATERIAL

Make sure that the size of the holes in the wire run is sufficiently small, preferably no bigger than 2.5cm, so that your chickens can't stick their heads out. For a stronger run try using 'weld mesh' instead of conventional chicken wire. It is made from thicker wires welded together. When choosing a chicken house and run, be aware that if the sides of the run are not vertical, the chickens cannot really use the area at the edge of the run without rubbing their combs against the wire.

FOOD AND WATER

Chickens like variety

Instinctively good at foraging, chickens are quite capable of finding a good proportion of their daily intake of food if they are given enough space and a variety of surroundings. They will eat grass and other greenery, worms and insects, as well as finding water in empty flowerpots and puddles. However, laying an egg takes a lot of energy and as such it is a good idea to provide a laying hen with the correct balance of protein, carbohydrate, vitamins and minerals, especially if she is not allowed complete free range. The best way to ensure she gets this is by using a specially prepared feed for laying hens.

Be consistent with the feed

A fully grown chicken needs about 130g of feed a day. Chicken food for laying chickens is called layers mash or layers pellets. They are a mixture of wheat, barley, oats and maize. A good quality feed will contain soya and not other forms of protein, and it should say on the label that it is vegetarian.

Layers pellets are the same as mash except that they have been formed into neat cylinders and are very easy for the chickens to eat. If your hens are confined to a run, it is better to feed them mash as they will find foraging for this more interesting and will normally split up their feeding times with other activities. You should store the food somewhere sheltered so that it doesn't get wet.

Grit

Pellets

Mash

Clean water is important

It is very important that your chickens have a supply of fresh clean water. You should refill the container every day, and in especially hot or cold weather

Above: These fountains work on a vacuum principle that maintains a constant water level.

check it at least twice a day to make sure that the hens have water to drink. On a hot day a single chicken can drink around 500ml of water. You can use either plastic or metal containers – look for ones which prevent the chickens from being able to tip the water out or stand in it, and make sure that they are durable and easy to clean.

Below: Chickens cannot swallow liquid in the way that we do – they have to tilt back their heads to drink.

HANDY HINTS

EXTRA TITBITS

You can supplement your hens' diet with scraps from the kitchen. Left-over cooked pasta and rice, as well as vegetables and fruit, are usually enjoyed. The best option is to experiment with different scraps to see what they like, as they can be quite fussy. Avoid feeding them any salty, sugary or fatty foods, citrus fruit or meat.

Pasta

Broccoli

Rice

GRIT FOR GRINDING

Chickens don't have teeth and can only digest food by first grinding it up in their gizzards using small stones that they pick up from the ground. If they can't find stones in their surroundings, you must supply them. Leave a container of grit in the run for the chickens to take what they need.

FOOD FOR YOUNGER CHICKENS

If your chickens are not point of lay (old enough to be about to start laying) then you will need to feed them a different feed called growers pellets or mash.

PREPARING YOUR GARDEN

Size matters

When you start thinking about getting chickens, you must make sure that the number of birds you buy is right for your garden. However much you want to keep chickens, a window box is not suitable! As a rough rule around 50 square metres for two birds is sensible, so it is quite possible to keep chickens in many town gardens. With this much space and a mixture of ground types, your chickens and garden plants will happily co-exist.

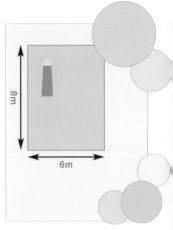

Above: An area of around 48-50 square metres in a garden is ample space in which to keep a couple of chickens.

Suitability

If your garden has perfectly manicured lawns and tidy flowerbeds, you must prepare yourself and the garden for a little bit of messiness. So what do chickens like in the garden? They love scrubby areas with bushes and shrubs to hide and shelter under. Chickens clean themselves by making a dustbath so your chickens will enjoy areas of loose earth, such as the back of a flowerbed. If you there is nowhere obvious to take a dustbath they may well

Above: Hens are opportunistic feeders enjoying worms, insects, seeds and greenery as they forage.

scratch a bath into your lawn – be warned! Chickens are not housetrained so they will poo all over the place. Chicken manure is great mixed into compost but can be too harsh and caustic if put straight onto plants.

Left: Chickens and pristine lawns do not go together. An area of rough grass like this is a better option.

Above: Chickens offer their owners much more than just free eggs; they also bring a garden to life as they scratch and potter around in the beds.

Chicken proofing

A two-metre fence will keep them in nicely, but remember that although chickens don't fly, they can do some impressive powered jumps, so anything left near the fence will enable them to hop up and over. Chickens love to nibble at new shoots and can be a real pest in the vegetable patch.

To prevent this you can section your precious seedlings off with some flexible fencing or use smaller wire cages to protect individual areas. Encourage the chickens to make a mess where you want them to by giving them an area of rough ground with bare earth to forage in.

Above: Keen gardeners may decide to erect some protective netting to keep their birds away from any specially prized plants.

HANDY HINTS

HAZARDOUS CHEMICALS
If you must use weedkiller or other chemicals, such as slug pellets, in the garden, make sure that your chickens are kept well out of the way. Don't let them back into the treated area until you are absolutely sure that it is free from these potentially lethal hazards.

FLOWERPOT DUSTBATHS
If you have a small garden and don't have anywhere for your chickens to dustbathe, a large flowerpot full of sandy earth can do the trick. Not only does it allow them to clean themselves but it is also very amusing to watch.

WATCH THE WATER
Chickens can't swim! Their feathers tend to soak up water rather than causing it to run off like it does from a duck's back. Chickens will probably just drink from a pond rather than trying to swim, but it pays to keep your eye on them the first few times they approach one.

BUYING A CHICKEN

Where to find chickens

It is unlikely that your local pet shop will sell chickens. Try instead the classified adverts in your local paper, specialist magazines and asking your vet or a local supplier of chicken feed. If possible, it is always better to go and see the chickens for yourself in their surroundings and you can ask the seller any questions you might have. Choosing chickens that have been reared together and are of the same age should ensure that they are already good friends and unlikely to fight. Before you go along, you should decide how many chickens you want, whether you can keep a cockerel and if you want a chicken that will be easy to look after and lay lots of eggs (a hybrid or crossbreed) or a pure breed that looks exotic but will require more attention.

What to look out for

A healthy chicken will have bright eyes, glossy feathers and be perky and active. A pullet will not yet have a big red comb, this will develop when she begins to lay. The legs should be smooth and the breast firm. You should check the bird's beak and avoid any that have a discharge; watery eyes and a dirty vent area are also signs that the bird is not 100 per cent fit.

Glossy feathers

Active and alert demeanour

Bright eyes

Beak clean, nostrils free of discharge

Firm breast

Is vent area clean?

Legs should be firm and smooth

Above: It is a good idea to visit the breeder and check a bird over before you decide to buy it.

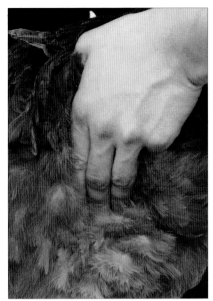

Right: One way of establishing whether a chicken is in lay (i.e. mature enough to lay eggs) is to measure the distance between its pelvic bones, as illustrated here. A bird that is in full lay should exhibit a span that is three fingers wide between its pelvic bones.

Below right: A pullet is a young female chicken that has not yet laid an egg. Pullets typically have smaller combs than mature females.

What age to buy

Adverts may describe a chicken's age as being at point of lay – often abbreviated to POL. This means that the chicken is about to start laying but doesn't necessarily mean that this will be the chicken's first laying period. You should always ask the age of the chicken as some people will sell their chickens after two years to make room for new hens. A chicken that has not yet laid an egg is called a pullet. It is possible to tell the sex of some crossbreeds at just a day old, while others can only be reliably sexed when they are at least four weeks old. Ideally buy your chickens when they are at least 16 weeks old as at this age they can still be tamed and there can be no doubt as to whether or not they are male or female.

THE FIRST DAY AT HOME

Bringing your chickens home

You can transport your hens home in a spacious cardboard box, lined with straw and with holes cut in the side for ventilation. Alternatively, you could use a wire pet carrier such as you would use for a small dog. Make sure that the container you use has plenty of ventilation; you can cut holes through a cardboard box for this purpose but make sure you do it before you put the chickens in the box! On long journeys check that the chickens don't get too hot, warning signs are panting and trying to cool down by spreading their wings. You should stop every couple of hours to give them some water.

Other pets

As a general rule chickens get on fine with other pets, such as cats and dogs. Try to let your chickens settle in for a few days before introducing them to other family pets and make sure that you only introduce them gradually when they are safely inside their run. Initially the chickens may flap around making them even more interesting for an inquisitive dog, but given time they will usually get along fine in the garden, pottering around with a healthy respect for one another.

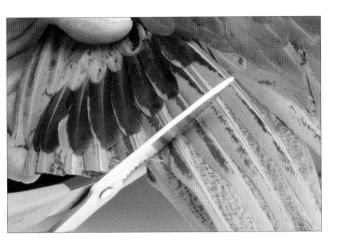

Wing clipping

Although most chickens are unable to fly high or over long distances, it is quite common and painless to clip their wings. It is only necessary to clip one wing to unbalance the chicken and prevent it from being able to fly onto or over fences. The person you bought your chickens from may have already done this for you. Alternatively, ask someone to help you by holding the chicken while you trim the long primary flight feathers on the edge of the wing. Using scissors cut the first six or seven feathers back to the point where the next line of feathers starts.

Above and top: Wing clipping is a simple and painless way of preventing your chickens from fluttering out of an open run or coop. Just clip the primary feathers on one wing, so that the bird is unbalanced in flight.

HANDY HINTS

EGGS

Eggs are full of goodness

The eggs from your own chickens are really fresh and a brilliant source of energy. An average egg contains about 70 per cent water, 10 per cent protein, 10 per cent fat and 10 per cent minerals. They contain all eight of the essential amino acids, plus vitamins A, B, D and E to keep your body healthy. The amount of protein in a single egg is equivalent to 14 per cent of the recommended daily allowance for an adult. The whole egg contains about 75 calories with around two-thirds of this contained in the yolk.

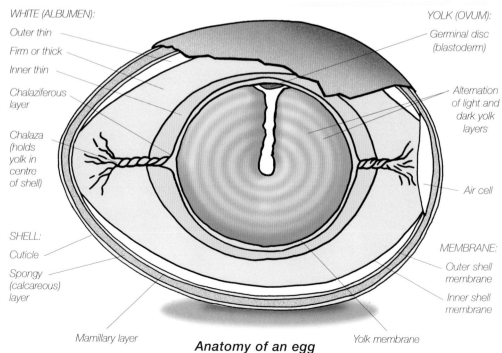

WHITE (ALBUMEN):
Outer thin
Firm or thick
Inner thin
Chalaziferous layer
Chalaza (holds yolk in centre of shell)

SHELL:
Cuticle
Spongy (calcareous) layer

Mamillary layer

YOLK (OVUM):
Germinal disc (blastoderm)
Alternation of light and dark yolk layers
Air cell

MEMBRANE:
Outer shell membrane
Inner shell membrane

Yolk membrane

Anatomy of an egg

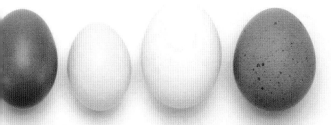

Size and shape

The first eggs that your chickens lay might well be surprisingly small, even as small as a grape. They will get bigger though as the chicken's body adjusts and develops until she is consistently laying eggs weighing about 60g. Your chicken may well lay some rather peculiarly shaped eggs over the years, from rough patches and long thin eggs to ones that look more like scrumpled-up balls of paper! The cause of the irregularities could be the chicken having a fright or just old age.

Eggs – one of nature's most amazing feats of packaging.

Number of eggs

The number of eggs that your chickens lay depends on the breed. Some crossbreeds can lay over 300 eggs a year whereas the most a pure-breed hen will lay is around 250. Because chickens are sensitive to the number of hours of daylight, they lay more eggs in the summer than in the winter. If you have two crossbreed hens, you will get around 12 eggs per week in the summer whereas in the winter this will reduce to eight eggs. A drop in the number of eggs your chickens lay is also one of the first signs that they aren't completely happy.

HANDY HINTS

COOL STORAGE
Eggs don't need to be kept in the fridge. If you keep them pointed end down in a cool place like a larder, they will last for up to three weeks. If you are not sure whether an egg is fresh, put it in a bowl of water; if it sinks it is fresh, if it floats it is rotten.

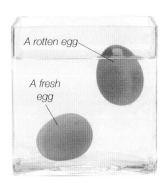

A rotten egg

A fresh egg

YOLK COLOUR
The colour of the yolks in your chickens' eggs depends on their diet. The more greens they eat, the yellower the yolk will be. Some other foods affect the yolk's colour; for instance, a few acorns can give it a greenish tinge.

SOFT EGGS
Weak shells can be caused by a lack of calcium in your chickens' feed. You can buy special poultry grit to remedy this, but an alternative is to bake old eggshells, grind them up and mix these into the daily feed ration.

CHICKENS' DAILY ROUTINE

Morning

Your chickens will have had a completely inactive night simply holding on to a perch with their eyes shut. As soon as it gets light, they will be awake and ready to be let out to start feeding. Assuming your chickens are more than about 18 weeks old, they will probably lay an

Above: In the morning your first job will be to let the chickens out to start foraging for food.

egg in the next few hours. If they live in a house with a nestbox, they will make themselves comfy in it, then stand up 20 minutes or so later having laid an egg. If you let your chickens out free range, then the next part of your day will consist of a hunt to find the eggs!

Daytime

Chickens will eat most of their food in the morning so make sure that they have plenty of layers mash to fill up on before you give them any treats. Eating will be followed by a good preening session. A dustbath will allow sand and earth to filter through their feathers so dislodging any mites. If it's a hot sunny day, they may well lie outside looking like they've melted with one wing outstretched! The rest of the day will be spent pottering round scratching for bugs and tasty morsels.

Left: Chickens that are contained in a run will normally disappear back into the nestbox area to lay an egg.

Above: If you keep two chickens, you can normally expect to harvest two eggs a day from them during the summer season.

End of the day

A very useful habit of chickens is that they never fail to go and roost at dusk. Make sure that you remember to leave the chicken-house door open in the evening. If they are ready to go to roost and find they can't get in, they will make a bit of noise and then find alternative accommodation. This is likely to be an unprotected branch which will leave them vulnerable to ending up as a fox's night-time snack.

Left: If you allow your chickens to wander around free range in the garden, you must be prepared to search around to find their eggs, as they will not necessarily use the nesting boxes in the chicken house for laying.

HANDY HINTS

CHECK FOR EGGS
Don't forget to go and check for eggs at around 11 o'clock. If you forget to collect your eggs for a few days. you run the risk of your chickens going broody. This behaviour can last for six weeks so it is well worth remembering to check for eggs daily!

DROPPINGS
Make sure that there aren't too many droppings in the house. As a general rule, weekly cleaning is enough, but a build-up of droppings can make life very unpleasant for the chickens so a quick daily check will be appreciated.

Above: Chickens appreciate a sunshade during hot weather.

WEATHER WATCH
If you keep your chickens in a relatively small run and the weather is at all extreme, snowy or sunny, spare a thought for their welfare. In both conditions they will be glad to have some extra shelter.

SEASONAL TIPS

Keep them cool, keep them dry

Most breeds of chickens are hardy and can live happily outdoors all year round. However, you must provide them with shade and shelter from the sun, wind and rain. The different seasons will affect how active your chickens are and the number of eggs that they lay. Although they will be less active in the winter, they will make the garden a brighter place all through the year as they provide visual interest and attract other wildlife.

Above: Chickens perform a useful job in the garden picking up pests, but they can be tough on young plants.

Spring and summer

Chickens are sensitive to light and so in the spring and summer they will rise earlier and go to bed later. The longer daylight hours will also encourage them to begin laying if they have taken a break from this over the winter. On long hot days chickens will be thirsty, so check regularly that they have enough water; you could put extra containers out too. If you let your chickens roam in the garden, they will pick off pests like slugs and flies. You may want to protect young shoots, however, as chickens can be quite partial to tender young plants. Depending on the breed of chicken, they may go broody in the spring or summer; to prevent this make sure you collect the eggs regularly.

Autumn and winter

Chickens, protected by their feather overcoats, don't mind the cold at all but they prefer not to get wet. As the weather turns, your chickens may spend more time under cover. If they can't find this outside, they will stay in their house. Covering the run to keep them dry and shaded from the wind will encourage them out to feed. You should check their water regularly for freezing, and use an old string bag to hang greenery in the run for the chickens to peck at. You will get fewer eggs in the winter because of the shorter days and some pure breeds may stop laying altogether. In very cold weather it is a good idea to rub vaseline into the chickens' combs to protect them against frostbite.

HANDY HINTS

LONGER NIGHTS
Don't forget that as the days get shorter, your chickens will go to bed earlier and that you will need to shut the door to their house earlier.

MIND THE MUD
Some pure breeds with long feathers will get very muddy and their feathers can get damaged if they are kept in muddy conditions in the winter. To prevent this, keep them on a surface which drains well, like bark chippings.

SAFER INDOORS
If you or your neighbours like to celebrate bonfire night or special events with a firework display, it would be best to bring your chickens into your house. You can put them in a spacious cardboard box lined with straw and with plenty of air holes and then pop them back into the garden in the morning.

GOOD MANURE
Chicken droppings can be put on the compost heap where they will help to make a very rich compost mixture that will improve the soil in your garden. The manure can even be put on some plants neat – it is especially good for currant bushes – but take care; it is too strong for most flowers and will burn them.

Left: In freezing conditions, a dab of vaseline rubbed onto the comb will protect it from the cold.

KEEPING THINGS CLEAN

Weekly care

Weekly care is principally based around cleaning the chicken house and making sure that there is not a build-up of droppings. Remove and replace any soiled straw or shavings and scrape out any droppings from the house. This is much simpler if your house has a droppings tray of some variety. Putting down some sheets of newspaper

Wood shavings

Chopped straw

or cut-up cardboard boxes stops the droppings sticking to the floor so making it easier to lift the soiled mess out. Also make sure that your feeders and drinkers are thoroughly cleaned out to prevent any bacterial build-up.

Both left: If your house has a removable droppings tray, it is a simple job to slide it out and hose it clean. Remember that the droppings make a valuable addition to the compost heap where they can rot down.

Disinfecting and mite powdering

However clean you routinely keep your chicken house, it is important that you perform a really thorough clean about every four months. Firstly do your usual weekly clean. Now take out any loose parts, roosting bars, droppings trays etc. Using a pet-hutch

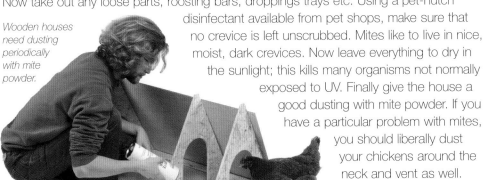

Wooden houses need dusting periodically with mite powder.

disinfectant available from pet shops, make sure that no crevice is left unscrubbed. Mites like to live in nice, moist, dark crevices. Now leave everything to dry in the sunlight; this kills many organisms not normally exposed to UV. Finally give the house a good dusting with mite powder. If you have a particular problem with mites, you should liberally dust your chickens around the neck and vent as well. This should ensure you a problem-free chicken house for several months.

Above: Perches and roosting bars need a brisk scrub from time to time.

House maintenance

Wooden houses need to be treated with preservative to keep them from rotting. Make sure your chickens are kept well away while you are painting the preservative on. Firstly check that none of the house has rotted and needs replacing, then follow the instructions on the packaging. Try to treat your house in the morning so that as long a period as possible can elapse before the chickens need to go back inside. If you have a plastic house, maintenance is much simpler and basically just involves a thorough clean with soap and water.

Above: Chopped straw is a convenient material with which to line the nesting box. It is easy to spread, and easy to dispose of when soiled.

HANDY HINTS

FOOTBATHS
Quite often your chickens can accumulate mud on their feet that can turn into hard balls. Soaking them in warm water will soon see the mud fall away, making your chickens much more comfortable.

NEST MATERIAL
You can use straw or wood shavings as nesting material. If you use wood shavings, however, make sure that it is manufactured specifically for the purpose. The wrong sort of shavings may contain very fine dust that can cause respiratory problems among poultry.

FEATHERED LEGS
Light-coloured birds or long-feathered breeds such as the Pekin bantam can get extremely dirty in the wet winter months. To clean the feathers use warm water and a little soap. Make sure you rinse them well and gently dry with a towel and some mild heat. Not too hot though, as you can damage the feathers.

HOW TO HANDLE A CHICKEN

A handful of treats gains their attention.

Building up trust

The first few times you let your chickens out of their run, do it in the early evening so they won't stray far. Stay in the garden with them and entice them to come close to you by scattering treats like sweetcorn and raisins on the ground for them to find. You can encourage them to come to you by talking to them and holding out food in your hand. When your chickens are happy to eat from your hand, then you can try to stroke them. Avoid fast or sudden movements and gently stroke the feathers on their chests and back.

Above: Feeding by hand allows chickens to grow confident of being around you.

Picking a chicken up

The next step is to pick your chicken up – be confident and bring both hands down over her back holding the wings against her body so that she can't flap. Lift her from the ground and hold her against your body supporting her underneath with one hand; she may struggle a bit but should, once she feels safe, be quite happy to let you hold her.

Use both hands to take a firm hold of the body and to stop the wings from flapping.

Left: Try to pick up a bird for the first time while she is calm and unflustered by your presence.

Difficult to catch

Try not to fluster your chickens by making wild sweeps to catch them. Chickens can move quite quickly and if you try and grab your chicken in a desperate lunge you may end up by pulling feathers out. If it is proving difficult, leave them alone for a few minutes to calm down before trying again later.

Sometimes it is helpful to have more than one person present so that, between you, you can block off all the escape routes more effectively!

Right and below: Once you have picked a chicken up, hold it against your body using one hand to support it from underneath. In this position, it is relatively easy to keep the chicken quiet.

HOME TO ROOST
Initially you may find it simplest to handle your chicken when she has gone to bed. Open the door of the house and lift her off the perch. Put her back gently. You both should find this less stressful.

Above: Tame birds can pop up in the most surprising way!

AN OPEN INVITATION
When your chickens have become tame you will find that they follow you about in the garden and may even hop onto your lap or shoulder if you sit down. If you leave the backdoor open, you may even find that your chickens pop in to have a look around your house.

This 'head reversed' position is also very effective.

51

CHICKEN BEHAVIOUR

Below: Every henhouse will have a pecking order which establishes the hierarchy within the group of birds. New introductions or young birds have to find their place.

Pecking order

Any group of chickens will have a pecking order. If there is a single cockerel amongst the group, he will naturally be in the top spot with the females forming an orderly queue behind him. If there is no cockerel, then the chickens will work out their own order with what can be vicious pecking and squabbling. The bigger the group, the more complicated and drawn out this process will be. Unless one hen is being badly picked on, do not interfere as – even if it takes a few days – they will finally sort it out and go on to live in harmony with each other. Introducing a new bird or taking a chicken away can trigger the whole process again.

Broody hen

From time to time your hens may go broody even if you don't have a cockerel. You can tell if a chicken has gone broody because she will stay sitting in the nesting box and be quite grumpy with you if you try to move her. It takes 21 days to incubate eggs but even if you take any eggs away from a broody chicken, it is not easy to snap her out of this spell. You should make sure that she has access to food and water but if she doesn't come out once a day to feed and drink, you should lift her off the nest and put her outside.

Above: When a chicken is about a year old, she will start to lose her feathers. Don't panic – she is not ill; moulting is a natural process of feather replacement that takes about six weeks.

Moulting

Once a year your chickens will moult. She will lose a lot of feathers from all over her body starting from behind the head, moving across the back and then down across the wings. She will look quite bald and then like a porcupine as the new feathers begin to grow through – they look like short, hollow tubes which you can see poking out through the skin. She will not lay any eggs during the moult and it will last on average about six weeks.

HANDY HINTS

RE-CLIP HER WINGS
Remember to clip your chicken's wings again after she has moulted and re-grown her feathers as the new flight feathers will enable her to take off. If you notice your chicken is losing feathers, check her to make sure that there is not another reason other than the moult.

When feathers grow back, you will need to re-clip wings.

EXCELLENT MOTHERS
Some breeds go broody more often than others. Bantams are very good mothers and are often used to hatch the chicks of other breeds who are not so inclined to go broody. Crossbreed or hybrid hens tend to be less inclined to sit and some will never go broody.

INTRODUCING A NEW CHICKEN
If you need to introduce a new chicken to an established group, you should do it slowly. Keep them apart but let them see each other during the day; at night put her in a separate house. After two or three days let them mix. There may be a short fight but the flock should accept the new chicken.

MAKING A
HEALTH CHECK

Keep your eyes open

Spending time with your pet is the first step towards ensuring that it stays healthy and happy. Just a few minutes every day spent observing your chickens is the best way for you to learn about their behaviour, habits and routines. Knowing how your chickens behave normally will make it easier for you to tell when one is ill or is in discomfort. Pick your chickens up regularly and give them a quick health check. If you do this daily, you should spot any problems at an early stage.

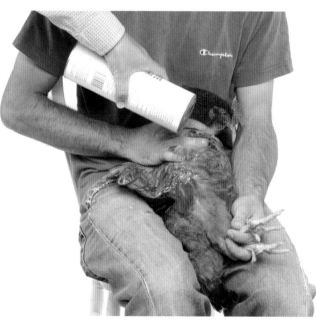

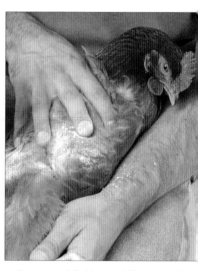

Above and left: Lice are biting parasitic insects that live on the chickens themselves. They can be treated by dusting with a proprietary powder.

Red mites

Red mites like to live in the small gaps and crevices which they find in wooden houses and are one of the most common problems encountered with chickens. They do not live on the chickens but come out at night and crawl onto them to feed on their blood. The effect on the chicken will be that she looks anaemic and stops laying. During the day you should check under the perches for mites. If present, they will be red, slow-moving and about 1mm long. You must treat the house with mite powder dusting it liberally over all the surfaces, paying particular attention to crevices and corners.

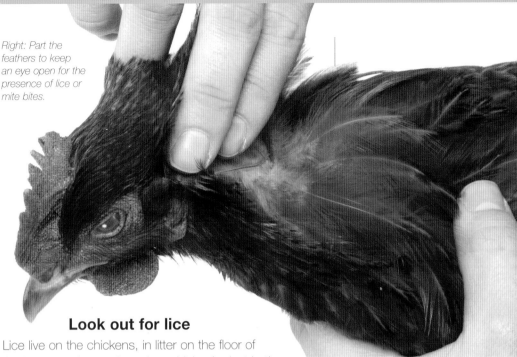

Right: Part the feathers to keep an eye open for the presence of lice or mite bites.

Look out for lice

Lice live on the chickens, in litter on the floor of the house and sometimes in a chicken's dust bath. You can check for them by parting the feathers around the chicken's vent and under her wings where you should see light brown-coloured lice and clumps of white eggs. They irritate the chicken and can cause feather loss. The treatment is to dust the chicken, the house and the dust bath liberally with lice powder until the problem clears up.

Scaly leg mites

If you look closely a chicken's feet and legs, you will see that they are covered in scales. These should be smooth and clean. There is a mite that lives under the scales which causes them to lift and come off. If you notice this, you can treat it by dipping your chickens' legs in surgical spirit twice a week until the problem is cured.

Left: Check your birds' legs regularly Scaly leg mites can lead to lameness.

LOOKING GOOD
The chicken's body should be firm but not fat, and her feathers should be shiny and complete; any bare patches may be a sign of lice or a skin problem. Most health problems with chickens arise from poor hygiene in the house or from keeping too many chickens in too small a space.

WEIGHT WATCHING
Most chickens are good at regulating their weight and will not overeat. However, if you feed your chickens too many treats, they will not get enough exercise foraging for food, and will become lazy and not lay as many eggs!

FREE RANGE
If you clean the house regularly and allow your chickens access to fresh areas of ground in which to forage, you should rarely have any health problems to worry about.

HEALTHCARE

Worms

Chickens, like many animals, can pick up the eggs of worms when feeding that then hatch and live inside their intestines. Chickens that need worming will maintain or increase their food intake while at the same time laying less or even stopping egg production completely. Their combs will look faded – pink rather than red in colour – and their droppings may be runny. If you suspect that your chicken has worms, you should buy a worming treatment from your vet to mix with her feed. Some people worm their chickens twice a year just to be on the safe side.

Left: The crop is an enlarged area in the oesophagus where food is stored before it passes into the proventriculus. If the crop feels hard, it is possible that it contains a blockage.

Crop bound

Eating long grass is not good for your chickens and may result in a blockage in their crops. The crop will be visible as a large bulge on the chicken's chest. This will normally only be noticeable in the evening after a full day's eating. If you notice the bulge in the morning and your chicken is not eating, pick her up and feel the crop. If it is hard, then you may pour a little vegetable oil down her throat and massage the lump to loosen and break it up. If this doesn't work, then it is best to take the bird to the vet.

Chickens can catch colds

Check that each bird's beak is clean and the nostrils are clear. Chickens can catch infections from wild birds and any discharge from the nostrils could be a sign that your chicken has picked up a cold. You may also hear her sneezing or see her opening her beak to breathe, a sign that the cold has affected her respiratory system. If you notice any of these symptoms, you will need to take her to a vet for an examination; a short course of antibiotics usually clears up any respiratory problem.

HANDY HINTS

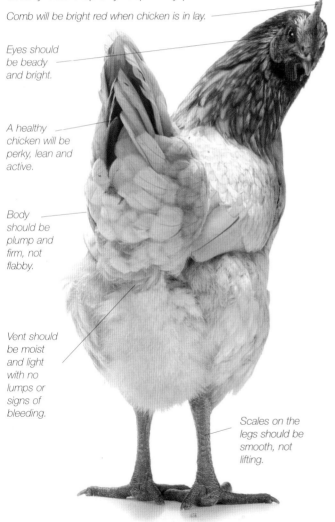

Comb will be bright red when chicken is in lay.

Eyes should be beady and bright.

A healthy chicken will be perky, lean and active.

Body should be plump and firm, not flabby.

Vent should be moist and light with no lumps or signs of bleeding.

Scales on the legs should be smooth, not lifting.

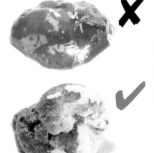

BREEDING CHICKENS

Hatching chicks with a broody hen

In a chicken run with a cockerel, the female chicken will lay fertilized eggs. In the spring or summer a hen may go broody and lay a clutch of eggs, between nine and 15 is normal, before sitting on them for the next 21 days. You should keep a broody hen in a separate house from the rest of your chickens. During this time she will turn the eggs regularly and move them about to ensure that the eggs are all getting an equal amount of heat. She will only come off the nest for about half an hour every day to feed, drink and take a dust bath.

Below: If you decide that you want to breed from your birds, you will need a cockerel to fertilize the hen's eggs. When she has laid her clutch of eggs, she will incubate them for around three weeks before the chicks hatch out.

Left: A broody hen should be kept apart from the remainder of your flock of chickens. A small garden ark like this is a convenient method of isolating the broody bird.

Hatching eggs using an incubator

Even if you don't have a cockerel you can buy fertilized eggs quite cheaply. They can be stored for up to two weeks and then be hatched under a broody hen or by using an incubator. An incubator is an artificial way of hatching eggs; it works by mimicking the action of a broody hen by maintaining a constant temperature and turning the eggs automatically every couple of hours. You should still check the eggs in an incubator regularly. It usually takes slightly longer than 21 days for the eggs to hatch.

When the chicks are born

If the chicks have been hatched by a hen, she will instinctively know how to look after her young. However, don't return the mother and chicks to the rest of your flock until the young birds are eight weeks old. If you have used an incubator, you will need to move the chicks to a brooder; this is a small enclosure with an infra-red lamp for warmth and food and water containers. After five or six weeks feathers should start to appear and you can take the chicks out of the brooder, but you must still keep them inside for another two weeks.

COCKERELS WILL NEED HOMES
If you have not kept chickens before, remember that you will need the right equipment to hatch the eggs and to look after the chicks when they have hatched. It is difficult to hatch chicks successfully and some of the newborn chicks will be cockerels for which you will need to find homes.

CHOOSE AN INCUBATOR CAREFULLY
It takes a lot of care and attention to hatch chicks successfully, especially if you are using an incubator. There are lots of incubators available and you should always read the instructions very carefully before selecting the right one for your circumstances.

FEEDING CHICKS
Chicks can live for the first 24 hours without any food or water but after this time you must give them special food called chick crumbs. Water should be provided in a suitable container that they can't drown in. If you have other pets make sure that they can't reach the chicks. If they are outside, keep them under netting so that they are not at risk from predatory birds like magpies.

GLOSSARY

Bantam Technically the 'bantam' is a type of fowl that does not have a larger version. There are nine 'true' bantam breeds. Many small fowl are referred to as bantams but they are actually 'miniatures' or a small version of a large breed.

Bloodspot An egg defect, caused by the rupture of blood vessels in the chicken. They are unsightly but still edible.

Broody The desire of a hen to sit and hatch eggs.

Chicken Technically the name for a bird (male or female) of the current season's breeding.

Cock A male bird after its first moult

Cockerel A young male bird.

Comb The red fleshy growth on the head of most chickens.

Crest The bunch of feathers on the head of some breeds.

Crop Part of the pre-digestive system of the chicken. Food collects here at the base of the neck and is softened before passing through the rest of the digestive process.

Cuticle The last layer applied to the egg in the hen's vagina. It acts as a barrier to disease-causing organisms.

Drinker A container for water that birds can drink from.

Dust bath Chickens will use an area of dry dust, be it earth or sand, in which to bathe in order to remove mites and lice from their feathers.

Ear lobe The fleshy part by the ears.

Flight feathers The largest feathers on the edge of the outstretched wing.

Gizzard The internal organ of the chicken that collects grit and aids the digestive process by grinding food down.

Grit Insoluble stony matter fed to chickens to assist the gizzard in grinding up their food.

Hen A female after her first laying period, roughly a year and a half old.

Hybrids Birds that have been genetically bred from two different breeds to embody good characteristics from both, such as laying well and having a good amount of meat.

Keel The bird's breast bone.

Meal A mixture of (wet or dry) coarse ground feed.

Moult The yearly shedding and replacement of feathers. It lasts for around six to eight weeks.

Pea comb A comb that looks like three separate combs, the middle one being the largest.

Pellet Type of food formed from a fine mash bonded together into small pieces.

Point of lay Term applied to a young pullet at about 18 weeks old, the age at which the bird could start laying. The first egg may not appear until four weeks after this however.

Primary feathers The first ten feathers on the wing starting at the tip and working towards the body. Out of sight when the bird is resting.

Pullet A female bird from the current year's breeding.

Pure breed A breed that is pure, i.e. it has not been crossed with other breeds or different varieties of the same breed.

Rose comb A wide comb that is nearly flat on top, and covered with small nodules ending with a spike. Its size varies with the breed.

Scales The horny skin tissue covering the toes and legs.

Single comb A flat vertical comb with serrations along the edge.

Vent The orifice at the rear end of the bird through which both eggs and faeces are ejected.

Wattles The fleshy appendages hanging down either side of the lower beak.

Wing clipping The practice of clipping, (cutting the ends off) the primary and secondary feathers on one wing to prevent the bird from flying.

A Wheaten Maran cock bird displays his fine comb and wattles to great advantage.

INDEX

CREDITS

The authors and publishers would like to offer their sincere thanks to the following people and companies who have provided valuable assistance during the production of this book: Robin Clover for the loan of the HandyHen chicken house pictured on page 26; Michael Neve and Joss Parsons at Denmans Garden, Fontwell for permission to photograph some of their fine collection of chickens and for assistance rendered during the shoot; Forshams Cottage Arks for the loan of the ark pictured on page 28; Eglu on pages 30-33,40,44-45,48-49 supplied by www.omlet.co.uk.

All the photographs reproduced in this book, with the exception of those listed below, were taken as a special commission by Neil Sutherland and are the copyright of Interpet Publishing Ltd.

Jane Burton, Warren Photographic:
2, 3, 58, 59 centre.

Fishers Woodcraft:
26 bottom right (both).

Forshams Cottage Arks:
27 top, 27 centre right; 28 bottom,
29 centre and bottom, 32 top,
36 bottom, 59 top.